Slim
Night
of
Recognition

Slim Night of Recognition

poems by

Emma Howell

A Lynx House Book
EASTERN WASHINGTON UNIVERSITY PRESS

12   11   10   09   08   07   1   2   3   4   5

Book design & typography by Karen "Maggie" Checkoway

Cover illustration: Edward Hopper, *Rooms by the Sea* (1951). Courtesy of the Yale
University Art Gallery, New Haven, Connecticut.

Author's photograph by Esmeralda Rupp-Spangle

Poems selected by Christopher Howell

Library of Congress Cataloging-in-Publication Data
Howell, Emma, 1981–2001.
  Slim night of recognition : poems / by Emma Howell.
      p.   cm.
"A Lynx House book."
ISBN 1-59766-022-1
I. Title.
PS3608.O953S65 2007
811'.54—dc22
                    2006036827

∞ The paper used in this publication meets the minimum requirements of
ANSI/NISO Z39.48-1992 (Permanence of Paper).

Eastern Washington University Press
Spokane and Cheney, Washington

Contents

v

TWO

Foreword

Emma Howell was born January 18, 1981, in Portland, Oregon, and died June 24, 2001, in the province of Bahia, Brazil. It was a short life by most standards, but the weight and content of that life were extraordinary. She was courageous, informal, disciplined, generous, and happy in the way only those who have fully understood their mortality can be. The genesis of this understanding is mysterious. Her time would be short — she seemed simply to have known this from an early age, and so bent all of her considerable energy and intellect to the process of becoming. She left behind many astonished and devastated friends, and the contents of this book — a body of poetry bright with darkness and joy.

From the beginning, in every aspect of life she sprinted ahead, announcing at age thirteen that she intended to finish high school in three years — though she decided instead to spend her junior year studying in Spain, where she augmented her Spanish with Latin and Greek. When she went off to Oberlin College, she again announced her intention to finish in three years and proceeded to take huge course loads, including the study of Russian, literature, and creative writing. But somewhere in that first year she became fascinated with Afro-Brazilian culture and put herself through an intensive ten-week summer course in Portuguese before going off for what was to have been six months of study in Brazil. She died in a swimming accident less than two weeks before she was due to come home.

She had been writing since the age of ten. This seemed natural: her relatives included accomplished writers and poets; her mother is an editor and book designer, and then there was me, her father, involved in writing and publishing most of my life. In addition to this seemingly hereditary predilection, there were writers around her constantly from the time she was born — the list of those who attended the party celebrating her birth included many of the best-known writers in the Pacific Northwest at that time. William Stafford, Vern Rutsala, Lisa Steinman, Henry Carlile, and her godfather Carlos Reyes were all there, and they remained part of her life, a kind of extended family.

So it was no surprise to discover that Emma was filling up notebooks, but she did not show me what she was doing and I did not ask to see it. Often, even at the age of twelve, she would engage me in relatively advanced theoretical discussions about writing, and she frequently borrowed books or asked my opinion of someone she had been reading. But I did not want to be someone who pushes his child to replicate his own vision of himself, so I resisted any direct discussion, or even knowledge, of her poems and stories.

The first poems I actually saw were published in a small magazine in Portland when Emma was fifteen. A friend showed them to me, shaking his head: they did not read like the work of a high school sophomore. They had a musical sophistication and a kind of muscularity, a sureness, rare even in the poems of college undergraduates. It was a breathtaking experience. Still, I did not tell Emma I had seen the poems. I thought I should let her decide when, or if, I was to become a part of her audience. Also, I did not know exactly what I would say if I were to be shown the poems. I thought of athletics and of those baseball coaches who critiqued their own sons' play so closely, held them to such a high standard of performance, they drove away all the pleasure their sons had taken in the game. So I waited.

For a few years, when Emma was in her teens, I taught one-weekend-per-month graduate-level poetry workshops, and Emma began attending these marathon classes, apparently with perfect comfort and unflagging interest. After a year or so, she began to offer commentary on the poems. The class was prepared to indulge her because she was my daughter but soon found indulgence unnecessary: much of her commentary, though she spoke neither frequently nor at length, was extremely perceptive.

I think it was these experiences that gave her the confidence to ask Henry Carlile if she could audit his undergraduate poetry writing class at

Portland State. Henry had never allowed a high school student into his classes before, but he looked at the poems and said yes. He later told me he thought her the best student in the class.

All of this accelerated Emma's learning so that when she did finally share her poems with me, just before she entered college, she was perfectly capable of processing whatever I had to say about them, responding to both criticism and praise with the passionate practicality it takes most writers decades to learn.

I say all of this not to prop up her credentials as a prodigy but to expose the depth of Emma's commitment to poetry and to language. The poems here collected, some extracted from notebooks she kept during the last six months of her life, speak absolutely for themselves, need no apology of any kind. She was the real thing. Poetry was for her a way of knowing and, next to friendship, knowing was what she liked best to do. The particular qualities of the work also need little discussion. Anyone conversant with poetry in the twentieth century will recognize in them the influence of the Spanish poets, particularly Vicente Aleixandre, and of the Portuguese poet Fernando Pessoa.

But such familiarity is really unnecessary. You don't have to have read a line of Pessoa or Aleixandre or Gabriela Mistral to feel the impact of these poems; the extraordinary directness of their emotional appeal, their sinuous musicality, their sensuousness and dark joy can only be escaped by not reading them. It is mature work, early work to be sure, but mature all the same. Among the many griefs that attend upon the loss of her is the grief that comes when one imagines the magnitude of the gift she might have brought the world had fate, or God, or accident allowed.

The other griefs are unspeakable. Nothing about our relationship can be replaced, and every day I wonder how I can possibly live without it. And every day, of course, I simply go on, for lack of a more viable option. For her mother, I know, it is the same. If Emma were here, she would tell me that this nexus of longing and the actual is important, that I should write toward it in a way that would help me fully experience its value, that solace surely lies only in our active attention. And so I do write, but the solace I find so far is a kind of mist, insubstantial. All of which is to say that I think she would be better at grief than I am, that she would integrate grieving, as she did everything else, because that is the kind of person she was: a whole one. She would remind me too, were she here, that all over the world children are dying, that I must, in good conscience, save some of my grief for them and for their parents, who are just as bereft as her mother and I.

I do not mean to suggest that Emma had no demons, but she was shedding them quickly, growing happier with every passing year, with every month, really, and in her last year discovered in herself a rich and mysterious spiritual life. More explicit than her love of literature and art, this discovery yet imposed no particular observances, but the drift of it, of her whole being, was toward embrace. The poems, particularly the later, longer pieces, show her feeling her way toward the numinous in herself and in life. She had found a path, and she left us this beautiful map, in case we might wish to follow.

Following it, in my editorial way, linking its loops and turns, has been excruciating for me. The knowledge that I would someday come to the end, the jumping-off point beyond which there would be no more poems, made me ache over each page of text. It is wonderful, therefore, to find in the completed book, more clearly than at any time since our last phone conversation on June 18, 2001, a living and beloved voice.

— Christopher Howell
Spokane, Washington, 2006

How beautiful upon the mountain
are the feet of the messenger.

Isaiah 52.7

ONE

Divination

History pauses, begins,
writes down the first word again,
creates a story, stringing
divination through the wings
and rafters of an old room
humbled, sealed with mud and loam.

Feathers dervish in corners,
nests cling to the eaves like burrs.

This could be anyone's home
forgotten by all its roads.
In a thick fog, history
expands the air, coloring,
drawing lead through dim windows,
lifting roofs high as gallows.

His Animal's Innocent Dream

The blue grate from the gutter
floats up to frame me,
make a boat of me
in the sea that is green with eyes
in the buildings that sail and change.
There are names, callings and benedictions
sent to the hidden voice
of a small boy or his animal's innocent dream.

My fingers have got dirty bringing me here
in their shell-like movements. I've arrived
but possibly not alone, possibly with a body and a mouth
with other bones.

I try to recognize myself in trees, but this green
aches and wails an unheard-of song.
I know there is a word for this in my body
or built into the ship I have become,
but I'm leaving it all: the hands for searching, feet
for when I get there, eyes for knowing which
dark island is my own.

I am rocking into calm, the perfect blindfold
I am humming and flying.
This could be the way, or could be the wave
that sounds just like home in its prayer
before sinking.

The Accident

I spoke with my baby mouth and gestured
with my hands and nodded
my sad breasts and bent my legs and jumped
the whole length of me and lost
my left shoe
and I sang a song I thought
I had forgotten.

The hands that surrounded me made bird
shapes and catcalls
purring me closer.
I arranged dolls on the dresser
and asked for a pumpkin supper
and wrote my father a letter
and before long the hours got dark and I was

singing that song I thought I had
forgotten
and it was the song of seeding
and all other work with the needle and thread.

Gravity

My center of gravity
is the gut and gape of me
is the swallow's pendulous
flight: empty, full, sips and gusts.

Sometimes I'm too full with words
to balance the wires and birds.

My mouth opens to catch air;
my body flags and fills with stars,
too heavy now, then too bright
to do anything but fly.

The south wind pulls my song out,
my arms spread to steady the sound;
I float down lightly, evening
humming — the world rises: coming.

It Is the Morning of the Day of Bleach

— for Galway Kinnell

It is the morning of the day
of bleach, mid-month, day after
payday   full moon   and we are
cleaning the house   gutting
the squash
preparing the soup for our
religion.
Soon we'll go down to the water
to salt our selves clean.
Meanwhile I set pumpkin with
gergelin to boil.   Meanwhile
I try to remember what my mother
showed me —
how lavender is the taste
of purity
and we grow it in boxes to remember
how we are little girls
and sleeping
still.
Something whispers, "This is the prayer
of safe homes."   I live all day
with *The Book of Nightmares* in my ear,

whispered toward my womb.
With nightmares my mother cradled
me to sleep. With nightmares I sing, I raise
the bread I will eat all week.
Between assaults I come in
and my empty home lays hold of me, shrugs
my bags off, unchains my feet. The house
whispers, "Calm yourself, eat your bread,
take your dose of nightmare sweet air."

In Praise of Sickness

My brother lives under water
and forgets things
in clockwise order, remembers in a way
memory can't support.

A woman in Texas believes
she thinks as animals do, that she holds
their wildness in herself.
She says her resurrection number matches
the number of teeth a shark will have
in its lifetime.

My brother assembles things
without directing them: marbles are rough oceans,
blocks are cities consumed.

The Texas woman says into microphones,
"There were younger times
when I did not know my name from the filth
around me, but the nuns brought me the night
the way I needed it. Now I believe

that all animals are instinctively female,
that they know the purity that darkness brings."

I wrap rosary beads around the mobile
hanging over my brother's bed
and watch the cross rock against the felt animals,
mixing their medicines.

Brothers: A Palimpsest

— for Caleb Hyde

How far we fall is directly proportional
to how much we've grown

since we broke the water
that kept us from gravity.

Night deadens in a kitchen of giant utensils. The useless
things I try to do with words —

grip the enormous ladle, stack 17 cups
end on end in a soup tureen,

try to make the eighteenth fit.

If I could call the runaway —
my brother — but he is untouchable.

If I could write to the runaway or our parents
and tell them the words that mean

I have planted their memories in my window
box with herbs and coffee beans — I remember

them clearly and with green hues
before they were running, I remember

them before they were broken
into the world to make me worry.

I remember them translated
smooth from breakfast to lunch

in one movement, in one house, by way of smoke
and the sunlight that made all things

thick and warm as bread
white and dim as fresh-cut canvas.

Foot & Moon

I dreamed me a mercy box and its weight in gold.
I am not beauty on the beach. I am imperial in my bikini.
I am bitten. My foot is poisoned and aches.
For all I know the sea planted its claws there to catch me.
There is not water enough to drag me drowned,
even weighted with wounds and riches as I am.
My guide is untouched by my dark breath, my weak and sullen
     panting.
My light slows and awaits me at the top of the hill,
there he rests with my father's moon.

Killing Time

You are the time between
when I waste myself,
when the rain stops
and there is no use.
You are demanding,
ragged hands,
talking into me
the "Yes, baby, please" of reason,
carving out of me
a keepsake
for your wall
that tells you what to remember
when you're blind.
Something holds me in,
keeps me close.
You are heathen and unclean
but I love your god-gorgeous sounds
in my head, many windows,
your hands, the only honesty:
our bed.

Letter to You the Day Before All Saints Day

Fall out my demon, fall out.
In the red net of my skin, be caught,
in the summer and the greenery
of my little woods where God
has touched me, be caught.

*

If I call you before you wake
will you dream me upside down
in the south,
hot and damp, my east bending back
for the cornfields we come from —

if I call you now with my white light,
will you wake from the north
and find me, waking backwards
into yesterday and waiting with my voice
for my steady tug on the sun?

*

(It is almost Pesach)

If I paint my door red
will the angel of death
pass by, will he let my first
breath be born?

If I slip into my green dress
and hold my smooth stomach in the bar
slinking in dance and alcohol —

and if I pray in the dark for blood,
whose angel am I?

*

Will you pray, dragging your prayer
east, pointing your mouth
at the sun? Will you light
the candles to guard me with fire
and remind my blood
every month of your absence?

*

Winter:
my skin under sleep like opium,
under your hand like china.

And now, January busted with color:
the welts of hard water,
the burns clutching my breasts
like starfish, my small chest
shining white under its red badge.

*

Fall out, my demon, fall out
of your polar night,

touch me in my little woods
and in my body shot
with morning, be caught.

Looking Alike

My eyes advance a steady pace
in the mirror, they try to leave the night in
the dark house of my mother's face.

But all over me the familial map is traced
in the parallelogram jaw and swollen chin.
My eyes advance a steady pace.

The fire of her crooked lip erased
my own bowed mouth. Lamps aren't lit in
the dark house of my mother's face.

Instead we burn photographs in the fireplace.
She watches the flame on my young skin
as eyes advance a steady pace.

She says I am the blood of her faith,
in the shadows she sees living again
the dark house of *her* mother's face.

Her beauty is broken into thread and vein.
She means to patch and mend my face.
My eyes advance this steady pace.
I'm the dark house of my mother's face.

Me Again

A former lover wants to draw me
and after a brickabrack of nerves
in the park we decide: with my clothes on,
absolutely. So we find his house
and I curve into an uncomfortable C
on the bed, near the wall, lift my chin
and wait two hours.

I am facing up, finding this
someone of shined copper joined to me,
so brilliant I go blind but do not
look away.

And this life against my life to be reckoned,
reasoned, demands my life
against the flight line of her mouth, my jaw
a wing against the hard exclamation of her
hands set to hips, symmetrical as blooms.

In a strange chemistry of memory
I exchange my eyes for a flash.
Fifteen years later I trade my mouth
for charcoal and the smooth throat of a bell,
its deep waist like worry lining the avenue of my body
with marigolds, those eternal borders of mourning.

A Midwest Death I

It takes a dream of luck to break a man,
to loose his jail of bones and send his feet
from dust and burns to lie in low cold lakes.

It takes a dream of rich, soft-eyed life
to lead a man from home asleep. At night
he dreams of full corn rows that point their peaked
green heads upward — like prayers or spires — to beg
for him a son whose face is just like God's.

A Midwest Death II

I
Every year, in the Midwest, death
rises from the cornfields like a symphony
while young men dive, palms together into the ground
to reach a blessing of seeds gone
and come again, to drag up the lost
waters and years of drought repented.

II
Men dig ditches in the shape of their fathers
and plant in the center a green life,
rubbing their hands together in praise
of the hard song every man has sung.

III
In the Midwest men get naked and wait,
on the front porch with the laundry,
for the hum of pollen, the air full of dust
and ghosts that float through every town,
carrying all the tired men
off their feet to heaven.

A Midwest Death III

In the Midwest women carry babies halfway
until the night turns into wheat —
that kind of dark.

The fields reach up through time,
waiting for a gift.

Women come halfway
to the barren limits of earth
then go home to streets and lamps and God
knows what kind of noise.

Here, someone could grow feet from dry stalks,
a mouth out of dust and dark
and learn to walk back stingy light
of the highway
swallowing a voice that brings dawn
all the way to town.

After *Traveling Through the Dark*

You could have cut open the cold girl,
let her size drop
from the life humming against her
and rolled her, empty, into the river.

You could have cut open the full girl.
She left you a token, being so
in the middle of things, under your lights.
She meant, stopping there, to give you a chance.

You could have cut open the unlucky girl,
pulled out a breath and saved yourself.
There would have been work in the warming
of your mouth around charity and that hot new thing.

You could have cut open that old girl.
But you pushed the whole affair into the river,
took your inheritance early
and rushed into the light: speed of your unburdened life.

She waits now in the cold, her deep burn
glowing through the dark.

Postcard from the Island

Look, father, I've inherited
that loneliness of yours.
It grows like a misshaped gourd
until the world is remote
on its spiked vine and I find myself
in flight.
Look at my insufficient wings
like paper leaves, my suitcase carved
from the wind — the whole world
below me pauses for the sun
singing that one vague hymn. Look at me
trying to memorize the chorus
of lands between us.

Predictions

I will recount predictions,
siphon from my faith's dictation

a poem or dream, calling:
"I'll kill myself in spring."

I dream in rows: three fathers,
husbands, sons — who will father

my daughter? All I know is
he'll have a beard like Moses

and she'll have my mouth, curved
above the lip, dented with words.

She'll sleep; I'll whisper Plath poems
into our dark-cornered home,

curse Lilith out of my womb
and save the seeds of our food.

Self-Sufficiency

— for James Grabill

If I could see my father as he was meant to be,
he would be a man
inside a man — trying to own a simple life,
trying to buy a small house.

I dream he is a man giving birth to men,
laying them like melons in my arms or
laying them on me in strips like plaster,
making a mold.

I dream he is a man translated
from all sad languages gone —
the deep sea and farming reports of poets
broken into the world now dead.

He comes to me while I am writing
to tell me all men turn back
to wombs — it is all right to be alone,
someone will always touch you, coming in.

Where I am afraid of birth pain and blood,
he shows me the scar of my birth,
traces me umbilically back
into the earth's clay spoon.

I've gotten used to the delirious
rustle of the year shifting on its haunches.
All around me leaves whisper
the Shul for the dying.

He says he can smell autumn
waking the dead
to their own language, telling their stories
of weather, a woman uncovering at night.

And every night there is a new constellation
in my sleep.
Every hour I hear him counting
down the moon.

He could rain a season of leaves in me
if I could ask him in Hebrew,
ink or fire;
he would answer me

by bringing a man
out of a man
in his palm
and touching me with it.

Standing Still in the Sky

I taught that wind a lesson!
— Evan Howell, age 7

He stays away from the corners, knows something delicate
About the long board and thick smooth paper balanced on his lap.

He sits slim and bright in the mosaic of linoleum.
The kitchen, his mother, her big wooden spoon: a collage.

He lines marker on marker, rolls pink orange black green blue
Into his own *arco iris*. He pulls the black and draws

Two tornadoes: one long and thin, a shady wanderer
Like his own uncontrollable limbs, and one wide and steady

As undeniable as his first home, that Kansas with peppers,
Long roads, and bright day lilies.

Between tornadoes a giant pink sea snail stalls
Like an airplane, holding still between time zones.

Music begins and lawn mowers, bees and bells:
A storm of ordinary noise surges through the red door

And spirals through the kitchen. He covers his ears,
His eyes open like daisies, he waits in the sunny afternoon

For the deep alarm to end in his organs.
He prepares to hold things together.

His fingers grip to shelter his own small sound
From the impact of surprise, speed, exploding mouths.

When the storm passes he'll set out to rebalance the deaf world,
Weighting it with huge fuchsia skies,

Make ballast of thick, green bushes and branches
To collect what's torn and broken. *He'll teach that wind a lesson.*

TWO

Tempest

It's storming, pounding out there.
rain breaks and falls like the mismatched
halves of haloes.
Luminescent drops arc above the wind's dips and joints.
This is the division of virtues through their centers.
Whole waters submit, are split and capped,
sectioned like tangerines into mouth-shaped crescents
and then auctioned into thunder.

The rain marks its weight in deep
forgiving streaks.
The storm is tight around all things
and in rope fingers of light
water cracks into marbled, complex structures,
less like a chandelier, hanging vows above our heads,
than like the mezuzah we kiss when we step outside.
It shelters a scrolled blessing against leaving God
at home.
We break Him into pieces and carry Him along.

The Country of Absence

by Gabriela Mistral

Country of absence,
strange country,
lighter than an angel,
and a subtle sign,
the color of dead seaweed,
the color of mist,
it's the age of forever —
that unhappy age.

There are no pomegranates,
no jasmine growing,
no heavens
or seas of indigo.
I've never heard
that name of theirs.
So in a country with no name
I am going to die.

No bridge or ship
brought me to it.
Nobody told me
in islands or countries.
I did not look for it
and I did not find it.

It seems like a story
that I learned,
a dream of taking
and letting go.
My fatherland is made
of living, of dying.

I was born of things
that are not a country:
of fatherlands and fatherlands
that I had and lost,
of the creatures
I saw die,
of what was mine
and what went from me.

I lost mountains
where I slept,
lost orchards of gold
sweet with life,
I lost islands
of sugar cane and indigo,
but I can see their shadows
keeping close to me:
the way committees and lovers
make a country.

A long mane of mist
without neck or back,
and the sleeping sighs
I saw following me that,
in the wandering years,
become a country.
And in a country with no name
I go to die.

(translated by Emma Howell)

The Map

— for Matthew Hill and Rashida Bumbray

I look through all my skin
and find these new countries:

I trace the elemental tropic,
the one that spits mercury and gasoline
up through the bean plants.
This is the equator of our desert —
that which adds light to light
and gives the trees and earth
a hot dank breath.

When did I grow this desert
where the sea has withdrawn on either side,
the land crowning then pushing through?
When did I grow these peaked corn heads
in my chest, shucking their green nods to the wind?
When did I start the harvest
that dries and bares my bones and thighs?
When did I start these crop circles,
plowing the sleep that bags my eyes?

When did I grow this wealth?

I count gold coins in my fingernails,
dollar after dollar in my toes
marking me with my trade.

Every day I look with all of my burnt body
for a body
of water to soothe.

How do you build a basket of reeds?

I look through all my skin,
turning limb over bone,
climbing my body's complicated roads.

I am charting and traveling,
folding into my eyes the sun, climbing
each higher limb so I can plant my feet somewhere.
So I can map the land that I may never find again,
and the land that I may never come away from.

I braid my hair and darken my mouth
so the day recognizes me as one of its own,
so I can tattoo myself a map,
lay open this song and take, star by star,
my body into the night and fire.

What I mean to do, yes even in this dry land,
what I mean to do is fly
because I can see — having borne
a weight larger than myself into the tangled, resistant limbs
up high — I can see there is no line
dividing earth and sky.

It's just land, wheat rolling through us,
then air, clouds and God
knows what kinds of angels meet up there —
maybe the lost lovers and children of our low cities,
maybe the unborn breakers of oceans.

All I have to do is find the right skin,
my feather skin, and heft me up
into the world above this world
where a deep breath of tides is the only food.

But wait, wait, I am full of the land,
so loaded with the bones and breaks of my
lovers and friends,
so leaden with my own, so wait:
how do you make a basket of reeds?
Moses, Moses. How do I walk into the sky,
that promise of light and water?
How do I carry with me the empty
and the salted lands?

How do I salt myself, so I am smooth
enough to swallow whole with my seed?

How do I offer myself, my birth and barren crops,
into the hands of God
that turn into stars into God into bread?
There must be a trade between

oceans and constellations, between
seeds and stars, between
the borders of countries
and the mouths of hymns.

What do I take with me? Moses
tell me
what needs to be planted?

Someone just take me near to the water
and Moses will do the rest.
How do we build a basket of reeds, Moses —
Moses, how did you get a basket of reeds

down the long river that I cross and uncross,
looking for the skin under my skin
that will let me in to chart the deep earth
riddled with opening eyes of seeds,
plowing brows of potatoes,

beets of bruised and bent elbows,
roots of underground hair
binding us to the earth?
We ride the length of our flesh-leash
into the sky before we're snapped back
by wiry tendons, pounded into the dark
that we stem from.

And the sky, with its thousand flashing eyes, warns:
Listen to the instruction that beats in the dust and mud, girl.

And I hear it said:
If we lie low in the bright fading hay,
we will find a river.
If we pull the stalks of long grasses that lisp
the certain music of the air,
and line our laps in straight rows of these reeds,
cross and open and cross our legs

(God, how a braiding of stalks
sews a body back up!),

then
we will rock a life out
of rock and broken grasses.

Then
we will set a life to sail.

So this is how you build a basket of reeds,
Moses, Moses,

this is how we built your basket of reeds, Moses, Moses,
this is how you set a life to sail, Moses,
this is how it floats.

The Call

I get a phone call before midnight
so I know it can't be anyone I love,
they are stuck in the Pacific pull and shove
their sun slides over, taking on broken lights.
I've heard they've been bringing in the tide
all on their own hands — plus a net —
and water follows them into the wet
world with red autumn skin.

I am sure they've heard nothing of me,
of my struggle to set a new east,
a sun of cornfields made to march
in and out of town. Their stalks stiff with starch
refuse me again, again. Two times a day
I call them east, two times a day west they stay.

The Story I Tell

I walked home suddenly,
suddenly past the cherries
and halfway there I was dreaming
of your father, the ghost,
who begged me with spoons
and smiles and his gorgeous, shining
red beard begged me
to eat and sit down
                among the cherries
with your father and the bright fruit
glistening a promise somewhere of my song
that he can see (he says)
lying between my breasts and clinging
to the soles of my feet like a small light,
a dusk.
              I come gradually down.
After six blocks or so, I have sunk
into the grass around him
and he lying near, soft in the grass.
              We sit trading the support of our ribs —
I lend him mine to comb blossoms from his hair.
He places me in his ark
and sets me off to sail saying
we will meet again when the land
is clear, dry to walk upon.

And we will eat through his red beard,
past his grave bones
and into the cherries for years.

I dream that I can sing this to you
and I sing to you
again, dreaming
and almost make it home.

The Parallel Flight

My brother visits the old Spokane airport
with its double thin rows of twin
engines, painted blue or yellow, named Daisy or Grandpa.

He glides light under the wings
to avoid the stinging dangers, bees
that buzz the sun, and wanders a loop of wings,
touching under tails, bumping tires
and stop blocks with his rubber shoes.
Dizzy as a spun blade, he circles
and looks past the antique windows of cabs
to the sky.

His circuits seem an invocation, rounded
over and over until his dust becomes a night wind,
a tornado to take them all up: each twin engine joined
and my brother, with his own twin, flying.

Things to Do

Take bottles back to the market
and the ripe fruit back to the trees.

Grow flowers where the bees' nests pinched
and ate the ground with honeyed mouths.

Paint the walls that dust hue, that looks
like lots of love covered over.

Punch bread naked so its skin
is a hard bark before evening.

Remind the sleeping boy of sun-
rise and set his breath in long days.

Lay yourself down like a half-moon,
let the vagabond night take you.

Say round, palm-shaped prayers
for a life of all things already done.

Tide

"You don't understand me," she says
and it has to be true.
Nothing understands her; the furniture
doesn't fit her,
she's been out all morning howling her
high whistles, calling
door to door for the bed that could hold
her heart and head together.
But she keeps changing shape,
the hands that touch her come away ten times
larger and strangely familiar with every one.
They can't catch her and fly her,
she is already her own machine.
She takes them away,
those who go heavily with the luggage
of never coming completely home.
She'll build the house
only to ask it to lie neatly down, ask you
to roll windows into the ground as seeds,
unpack your body, shut and close and fold
you up for winter.
She demands of the traveler out loud
the sign to that private road,
asks to play island to all of them,
seasick, plays the moon, covers them
in direction and secret smells of arrival.

She will hold you in
to be understood,
to be fit and measured in each of your bones.
But she'll let you go, too.
So watch close your hands, your voice and road,
your fingers in their tight grip
go suddenly huge and dull as boulders; all
the things you've loved, let go as well,
come floating from you at a strange distance
with maybe their directions taken
even from themselves,
looking, at least, wholly foreign and unowned.

We Are Not the Sum of Our Parts

1. *Landscape with Lover*

The trees disperse,
their grey trunks multiply into a maze.

The ground is black
from rain, the leaves are yellow falling,

there is still new grass cutting
through the dark air, pointing

delicate punctuation at the clouds.

And outside the trees, the city
mulls and blinks its red yellow eyes;

all things move at this rate,
summer stops into autumn,

autumn slows into winter,
winter, once back,

pays no attention to the signs,
and freezes all seasons until a green,

rising up, arrests it,
points accusing arrows at the ice storms

and defends the small roots
by inflating those little chests of leaves.

2. *She Leaves for a Few Days to Breathe*

I bet she is riding a wave of air right now.
I bet the ground ridges under her, nuzzling
the soles of her feet. She steps between

the earth's spine-knobs and rib-hooks —
the skill of a foot finding footholds,
hands making handles of bird dives.

She fits her thought into the cracks
between rocks and her body follows.

Between ankles and earth,
between the ash ribbon of hair and the sky,
there is a quiet conversation of grace:

chin propped on the chinks of ledges of the air,
elbows flexed, arms shaped like sevens,
breath orbiting the wishbone,

legs braiding the world seen between legs
into a mat of reeds, eyes like a glass
of water before you drink.

What You Need to Know

1.

Once taken in the warmth of your room —
room blue as a flame on a burner —
you saw the sun rise a day too close
to the world
and light had its way with you.
After two such sloping hours you learned
that your father's are the only wings
strong enough for God.

2.

What nobody told you
will appear to you only after years
with the same dry body that puts you down
into her center, touching the only water
she has left.
The last atom remembers the sea
and your breath sounds like a shell.

So every month you ride her tide,
her body arches with travel
and your tongue burns
to get all her beauty out
in a song that floats, white, to the world.

Sustenance

This is me making my love
from the quiet slip and tug
of God shimmering out of us —
raw as prayer in early mass,
made from the green smell of tea
and the musk of dawn rising.

Or, love is nothing but what's
in our eating bowls, clay cups:
first, the food gathered raw, then
the hot flight to get past skin,
the simmer of bones and roots —
the earth offers up its soup

that outlasts, in its cobalt,
our season, that empty gut.

Route 14

We drove two hours the gypsy route
down canyons to the sea on an empty
radio of dead blue sky.

Our coast was invented by wanderers
and bringers of ice and magnets,
the rightful owners of our opposite poles.

In a tin mobility we rode
to discover the nomad paths,
their green histories of faith that hold

the mixed race of the ocean
and a chaste procession of the gypsies
of all the world.

Through a rainstorm we drove
from the tribe of questions, past miracles
born dark from our hands, our waters

long and heavy, weighing the migration
into seasons, our gypsy homes
shaking far away.

Leading Me

The feet that follow me are thin
and shining, smooth as feathers.
Even to the glass and the broken
they are angels from some wrong
turn in my body.
They return eye to eye
to help my heart out of itself.
These are the faithfully silent,
the hidden risings of necks
to the beaks of flowers.
These are the outcasts that tell me
not to show my hand.
Prayers fly back from their high place,
prayers that wait for spring
and prayers with blessings for ribs
stop here, with me
they become feet with each proper
bone.

I am under the road, part destination,
part monument halo rising up
through the cool mud
into air gone silver with speed.

I am an agent of the thing that follows
my faith's body, walking the slow rocks.
The trees praise and make wing
to point the way against a white

white music that marks the days.
Feet that know my feet
stain the horizon where I've been.

My thin follower, floating benediction,
our wings together make us whole enough
to touch the skies of grace.

Against Blindness

In me, the huge night package,
there's someone wanting to shine shoes
black and thick to the sole,
someone cooking only with red spices
and selling someone whose face is cold.

It's crowded here.
We hold our breath until day.
There is someone from every somewhere.
I can even touch you again
or go swimming in that dark

where we are always fish,
silvered with travel.

I go home.
Maybe you find a high plane
that sounds like a thunderstorm
before it comes.
We leave our fingerprints, a charm
against blindness.
We lace ourselves like leaves,
make a smooth net, a mirror, to catch
each day from the sacred dark
between each body.

The light, an exhale,
raises orange trees and water
like lizards to wade the sun.

We come in, opening
and closing our mouths like wings.
Swallows, we fly away,
lie down between breast bones
and the heart made night.

Just This

All I know I have said into an emptiness
to test the depth of it.
And all I have been allowed to keep
has echoed back to me by some divine
miracle of physics. This is the difference
between light and water — where one is the speed
of my life in heartbeats, the other is the dream
where I descend and visit the unknown treasuries
of my history. I am old in this dark place,
and the brokenness of my voice is the sound of time
flowing back to me, eating my words backwards,
hearing them before they leap.

When to stop? When to know which
word has entered its temple and locked me in?
How to recognize the sound of that shuddering door?
This is all the world, and in my sleep
there are older ones. In my sleep there are hands
like truck stops and railway stations, endless embarking
and disadventuring.
What I have learned from leaving: the smoothest
of my parts is like to be burnt.

What I have to learn from coming home: there is never
a home planted in the same day; all your years
make you new like clockwork.

Whatever was the tendency of love is now a rite
in some foreign customs office dark with abandoned things.

All I have given I have given over under a false name
because they are the things that will follow me, they are
the way I know how many people I have been and how much
each of them has cost. In my divine counting
all addition is minute, barely a second in the sun
and we subtract the whole night through.

My doubts pile like dust, full of its life of insects
and filth and all of this is the infrastructure of love,
I think. All of this the building up of the tower
toward God. And once again, when to stop?
When to break tides from shores
and wake. All the world is ebbing as I recite the miniatures
of this life: bestiaries, aviaries, Newton and mechanics.
Since when is there such burning, such barrage in the daily plait
and stamp of things? Since before the infancy of stars,
I think. And I answer myself by falling out of sleep
three months, twenty-three days, and eighteen hours long.
If there were ever a river drawing its carriage of little lives
to the sea, I am in it. Minerals. I think minerals
as I wake.

Prayer

At some point you pray
not because you've made it

not because you see the stony hand
opening before you
but because somewhere the sky leans a familiar grey
into the trees and they acknowledge it
reweaving the shroud of their deep roots.

Nothing particular happens in you —
the sky becomes a still white mound
and you find your knees suddenly wanting down.

On the Eve of the Winter Solstice
I Write to the Northern Hemisphere

Dearest:

It is likely I am faint
because my throat is dry and aching
and I am stripped hot in this rainy
unlikely simulation of winter.
It is south and June and dark and early, love,
love, everyone, father and professors.
These are the houses I came for.
This is the intrigue for which I unbuckled
two years of life well spent.
Let me be about roaming the tide
where crabs raise their warrior young
and break their shells on fishermen's teeth.
All of this is simple, a saltwater river
recounting my recipes:

> — *8 glasses of water left 7 days to breathe.*
> — *The screaming cats in the street kept clean with lavender and milk.*
> — *The begging children kept by a constant god of candy and smashed windows.*
> — *The sweet Portuguese of hookers in the early calm.*
> — *The dawn of day blistering with the fanfares of men on the way to work.*

My brother reminds me to keep clear of tornadoes.
They are the providence of his blue eyes
and deafening understanding of right
which is all around him for miles.

I think of south and close my house. Could this be
the breaking point? Could this be the prayer
nudged out of sickness and begging?

At night I hear the long wail of reassurance:
these are still my dreams and shivers
under the heat.
I hear everything tonight
and it seems a wind from far off
and from far off cocks crow their mournful
announcement to the world:
all is dark and lost. We cannot fly.
It is night and we are each and each
the bodies without dawn.
Where do I go from here?

I was meant for coherence, a solidity of sound and light,
be it the steady track of airplanes deepening
or a voice muscled in wind
or the truth of seasons laid clean, for once
all ritual and agony.

But the leaves don't fall in this country.

What do you know of distress, shore rider, foreigner,
miscreant? What do you know
of the bathings I take, the salt and sweet waters
that silver my repentance? Again and again
I fan out my lucky stars.

This is a season, only an age,
a recommended lapse in symmetry
to help God know that I, though unfaithful in memory
and in deeds, remember Him.

> — *Dip three salted fingers in the ash of a dying violet (remember Violeta africana) and finger out the roots.*
> — *Your tongue will want of sugar.*
> — *Your eyes will beg of water.*
> — *Wait for dawn.*

Twenty unshed years are the equivalent of five minutes
in the sun.

Slim Night of Recognition

I've been practicing
because it's all about the ritual.
Wrapping myself tighter
and looking for darkest corners because
you don't want the light
to find out what you've done.

There is a path of evolution
that can follow you anywhere
so you've got to watch your footing.
And there is no escape
when your intention is carved
in every bone and step
between you
and the inevitable avalanche.

The last rite
is the laying down,
the acceptance of lasts,
the becoming something less than whole.

Too slowly
the final appreciation of sky
before it rolls over
and makes your last word
one of the stars.

Acknowledgments

Some of the poems in this volume previously appeared in other publications:

The Dial:	"A Midwest Death I"
Enchiridion:	"Me Again"
Field:	"Divination" "Gravity"
Rain City Review:	"Slim Night of Recognition"
Rock and Sling:	"Letter to You the Day Before All Saints Day"
	"In Praise of Sickness" "Prayer"
Salt River Review:	"It Is the Morning of the Day of Bleach"
The Artful Dodge:	"His Animal's Innocent Dream"
Turnrow:	"Just This" "Foot & Moon" "The Country of Absence"
Willow Springs:	"It Is the Morning of the Day of Bleach" "Leading Me"
	"The Parallel Flight"

"Tide" and "Against Blindness" appeared in *Playing with a Full Deck*, ed. Dan Raphael (Portland, OR: 26 Books, 1998).

"His Animal's Innocent Dream" appeared in *The Poet's Calendar: 365 Classic and Contemporary Poems*, ed. Shafiq Naz (Bruges, Belgium: Alhambra Press, 2007).

Christopher Howell and Karen Checkoway would like to thank the people at Oberlin College, in particular Kay Coughlin and the Office of Development for their help in setting up the Emma Howell Memorial Poetry Prize Fund; and Pam Alexander, Martha Collins, and David Young of the Creative Writing Department, for the support and guidance they gave to Emma as a writer and to us in putting together this collection.